Hist...
C

www.dinobibi.com

Contents

4

Introduction

Celtic double headed monster bird pattern

No mythology is more magical than Celtic mythology. The Celts of Ireland, Scotland, and Wales created an imaginative world full of fairies, sea monsters, and nature gods. Sadly, most of their stories are lost, and the only things we do know are just bits and pieces of a larger religion that's gone.

Even so, thanks to medieval writers in Ireland, we know about some of the traditions of Europe, centuries before the Romans took over. Celtic mythology is important precisely because tales of the Celts and their religion have survived to this day. Even though the Romans tried to wipe out Celtic culture (which you'll learn more about in the next chapter), stories about their gods and goddesses still fascinate people all over the world.

You probably have one important question to answer first, though. Who exactly were the Celts?

Chapter 1:
Who Were the Celts?

The Celts were never just one group of people ruled by a king or some other type of politician. Instead, they were tribes that lived all over Europe during the Iron Age (1200 BCE to 550 BCE) and had similar beliefs. Most of the stories they wrote down were destroyed when the Romans took over, so there's not a lot we know for sure about the Celts. Some of the things they believed became Christian ideas or symbols. Archeologists have also been able to dig up some old relics that belonged to the Celts. Most Celtic tales come from medieval Irish literature.

One piece of Celtic culture that's still around is the language. There wasn't just one Celtic language, though. A different version existed in different tribes. The six Celtic languages that are still spoken today are Welsh, Irish, Breton, Scottish Gaelic, Cornish, and Manx. Cornish and Manx were dead languages for a while, which means there wasn't a single person on earth who could speak either one. Then, some people got together and decided to try to bring the languages back, so they started teaching kids. There are only about 100 people who speak each language now, but that's better than zero!

Modern sign in Welsh and English

None of the tribes called themselves Celts. As far as we can tell, the only people living at the time of the Celts who called them that were the Greeks. Their word for Celts was Keltoi, and they thought the Celts were backward barbarians. Back in the day, Greeks, Romans, and Christians called anyone who wasn't part of their society a barbarian, which means uncivilized. The Celts weren't uncivilized, though. They were just different, which was a dangerous thing to be in the past.

Where Did They Live?

United Kingdom countries and Ireland political map

The Celts weren't one group of people living in a certain area; they were all over Europe. Tribes lived mostly in Ireland, Scotland, and Wales, but they even stretched as far as Italy and Turkey. That's most of Western and Central Europe! The Celtic tribes lived so far apart that they didn't all believe in the same gods. Some of their gods even had different names but served the same purpose. The Gaels who lived in Ireland and Scotland, the Welsh from Wales, and the Celtic Britons who were from Great Britain and Brittany (in France) are the tribes we know the most about. The myths and stories from their cultures were written down a long time after the Celts were taken over by the Romans, so some of them might not be exactly the same as they were when the Celts invented them.

In this book, we will try our best to let you know where certain stories come from and which tribes believed in which gods and goddesses. Not even historians are sure about who believed in what, though.

What Was Life Like for Them?

The Celts might have been called barbarians by bigger civilizations, but they had organized societies, trade, and traditions that proved they were just as 'civilized' as anyone else.

Most Celtic tribes were divided into three groups. At the top were the nobles who were either kings or chieftains, depending on the tribe. After the nobles came the craftsmen and free people who were kind of like today's middle class. At the bottom were the commoners and farmers. Most societies in the past would keep everyone separated based on the jobs they had and how much money they made, but the Celts didn't. Chieftains could talk to commoners, and commoners could trade with craftsmen. Everyone worked together to make their tribe successful.

The Celts were skilled craftsmen that made some amazing things, including beautiful shields that archeologists have found. When you think of a shield you probably picture something round and small, but the Celts made long, rounded, rectangular, and oval- shaped shields that could protect their whole torso. The shields had beautiful designs on them. Sometimes, Celtic tribes would go into battle wearing no armor. They would bring a shield, a spear, and nothing else. They were fierce warriors, and tribes fought each other a lot to get more land or sometimes just for fun.

Several people dressed in the costume of ancient Celtic warrior

The Celtic Year

Times of the year were very important to ancient cultures. They needed to keep track of what season they were in so that they could plant crops and figure out when to harvest them. Many cultures came up with festivals and celebrations to mark different seasons and times of the year. The Celts did the same. Historians can't be 100% sure that the festivals we associate with the Celts were actually invented by them. They lived so long ago and there are no written records for us to go on, but we can make an educated guess. According to Irish folklore, the main four Celtic festivals were Samhain, Imbolc, Beltain (or Beltane), and Lughnasadh.

Samhain

Performers at the Samhuinn Fire Festival, Edinburgh

A lot of people still celebrate this day, but we call it a different name. Halloween! To the Celts, Samhain (pronounced sow-in) was the night when the veil between the living and the dead was so thin that spirits and people who were still alive could talk to each other. Just as not all people are friendly, not all ghosts are, either. The Celts would wear costumes to confuse angry spirits and light bonfires to chase them away.

Samhain was the time of the year when summer ended, farmers stopped harvesting, and winter was on its way. Since crops don't grow during the winter and it gets really cold, Celts associated this time of year with death. That's why this festival honored their dead relatives.

Imbolc

Brigid's Cross

Imbolc (pronounced im-bulk) celebrates the time of year when winter ends, around February 1st. It is also called Brigid's Day in Ireland because Brigid is an Irish saint. Many Celtic tribes raised sheep, and Imbolc marked the time when sheep would be ready to have babies, called lambs. Celts celebrated Imbolc as a way to ask the gods to make sure healthy lambs would be born.

Beltain (also spelled Beltane)

Beltain celebration

Beltain (pronounced either bell-tane or bee-yawl-tinnuh) is a fire festival that happens around the first of May. The name means "bright fires." To the Celts, the world came alive at Beltain. Flowers started to bloom, warmer weather was on its way, and brighter times were on the way. We still celebrate Beltain in a way, but we call it May Day.

On Beltain, cattle would be let out of winter pastures and moved to summer meadows. Before they were let into the summer meadows, they would be led in between two bonfires that were supposed to cleanse and protect them.

Some Celtic tribes also believed in fairies, what they called aos sí. These weren't nice, tiny fairies with glowing wings. The fairies

15

the Celts believed in were powerful nature spirits that could be very mean when they wanted to be. Part of Beltain tradition was to make sure the fairies were happy by leaving gifts for them.

Lughnasadh

This festival is associated with the Celtic god Lugh. You'll learn more about him in the next chapter, because he is very important. Lughnasadh (pronounced loo-nah-sah) is a month-long festival that starts two weeks before July 31st and ends two weeks after August 1st. It marks the end of summer and the beginning of autumn, which is when Celts would start harvesting crops.

The god Lugh was associated with skills like archery and horseback riding, so many Celtic tribes would celebrate by holding contests. They almost put together their own mini Olympic games, in a way. They had long jumping, spear throwing, wrestling, swimming, and many other competitions for warriors.

Some Celtic tribes would gather together for Lughnasadh to trade goods and news. Since fighting wasn't allowed during festivals unless it was part of the festival competitions, Lughnasadh was a rare time when Chieftains could get together and talk peacefully.

Celtic Druids

Costumes of Ancient Britons, Druids

We can't talk about the Celts or their mythology without mentioning the Celtic priests, known as druids.

Most of what we know about the druids comes from the information Julius Caesar wrote about one group of Celts who lived in an area called Gaul. The druids were like priests, teachers, and judges all in one. They were the most important people in Celtic tribes other than the kings or chieftains.

Anyone could study to be a druid. Apprentice druids learned about astronomy, nature, and stories of the gods. All of their training was supposed to give them the knowledge they would need to advise their tribe and give out wisdom.

In Gaul, druids would get together once a year to listen to legal cases from the tribe and make decisions on punishments or how to resolve situations. They also might have performed human sacrifice as a way to ask the gods for help or make them happy if the druids thought the gods had been angered in some way.

What Happened to the Celts?

The main reason we don't know a lot about the Celts (besides the fact that they didn't write a lot of their history down) is because of the Romans. The Romans wanted more power and more land, and they were willing to do anything for both. The Celts were not under Roman rule for a long time, and they didn't want to be. The Romans fought them anyway, wiping out a lot of the tribes and forcing the rest to convert to Christianity. Many Celtic traditions disappeared or were changed to fit into Christianity.

Some Celts who converted to Christianity to avoid being killed by the Romans held onto a few of their traditions and beliefs. Ireland and Scotland are two places where Celtic traditions are still strong, thanks to the Celts who didn't let outsiders get rid of every part of their religion.

Chapter 2:
Celtic Gods and Goddesses

Almost every Celtic tribe worshipped a different group of gods and goddesses. There were some commonalities, though. Most tribes believed in the gods and goddesses we still know about today, though under different names. When the Romans began converting the Celts to Christianity, they changed some of the Celtic gods and goddesses into Christian saints. This account is especially true of Brighid, one of the goddesses you'll read about in this chapter.

First, let's look at some of the gods that were present in one form or another in almost every Celtic tribe.

Gods

Dagda

Celtic meaning: "Good God"

Other names: Fer Benn, Dagda Donn, Eochu, Dáire

Dagda was the king of the gods and sometimes called the Father God. He was a god of manliness and strength since he was a fierce warrior. He was also very wise and was the god of the druids, who believed they received knowledge about the world directly from Dagda. Dagda was also thought to control the weather and have the ability to bring plenty of rains for a good harvest or cause a drought.

Dagda's weapon of choice is a huge club, which is kind of like a big stick with a larger rounded end that's used to hit things. Dagda's club can both kill people and make them come back to life. He called this club the lorg mór.

Club

Dagda also owned a cauldron called the Cauldron of Plenty because it always had food in it that never ran out.

Lugh

Celtic meaning: "The Shining"

Other Names: Lug, Lleu (Wales), Lugus (Gaul)

After Dagda, by far the most popular and widely worshipped Celtic god was Lugh. He was the god of arts and crafts, and some tribes also called him the sun god. Lugh was also known as 'Lugh of the Long Arms' because he carried a spear that never missed and was like an extension of his own arm.

Spear

Many places in Europe were named after Lugh, such as Lugdunum, which is now a French city, and Luguvalium, which is now Carlisle, England.

The festival Lughnasadh honored Lugh since he was associated with the sun. This festival was also a time for competitions and tests of skill since Lugh was the master of all skills. He was a poet, warrior, smith, carpenter, scientist, and everything else you could ever think of.

Maponos

Celtic meaning: "Great Son"

Other names: Aengus (Irish), Mabon (Welsh), Maccan Óc

Maponos was the son of Dagda. He was the god of love and youthfulness. According to legend, he always had four birds flying around with him wherever he went. These birds were symbols of his kisses, and he could use them to make anyone fall in love with him. He also made other people fall in love with each other.

Chapter 3 tells a beautiful story about Maponos using his Irish name, Aengus. In the story, the god of love finds his true love.

Cernunnos

Cernunnos

Celtic meaning: unknown, possibly 'horn'

Other names: The Horned God, The Green Man

Cernunnos was the god of the forest and protector of animals. Drawings and carvings show him with stag horns, long tangled hair, and a wild beard.

24

No one knows anything about Cernunnos except he was the nature god who lived in the forest and made sure all the animals and plants were taken care of. When the Celts converted to Christianity, Cernunnos's image was taken and used to represent Satan, or the Devil. He wasn't evil, though. He just liked hanging out in the forest more than being around people or other gods.

Belenus

Celtic meaning: "Bright one"

Other names: Shining God, The Fair Shining One

Most Celtic tribes celebrated Belenus during Beltain. The fires lit during this festival represented the sun and were made to honor Belenus and ask for him to bring the sun back. While Lugh was sometimes seen as the sun god, Belenus was the official god of the sun. He was also associated with horses and thought to move the sun across the sky using a chariot pulled by horses.

At one point, Belenus was the patron god of the Italian city of Aquileia. Archeologists have found evidence that Belenus was worshipped in more than 30 sites between Italy and Ireland. Belenus was right up there with Lugh and Dagda as being one of the most important Celtic gods.

Goddesses

Ana

Celtic meaning: unknown

Other names: Anu, Danu, Annan

Ana was the mother earth goddess associated with nature as well as prosperity. She was often called by the name of Danu and was thought to be the daughter of Dagda.

Some places in Ireland are named after her. The "Paps of Anu," a region of Kerry, Ireland, is named after her.

Sadly, we don't know anything else about Ana. She was most likely turned into Saint Anne when the Celts converted to Christianity, and anything that was known about the goddess wasn't written down or recorded.

Brighid

Brighid

Celtic meaning: "Exalted one"

Other names: Brigid, Brigit, Brig

Brighid was one of the most beloved goddesses in Celtic culture. She represented the spring, healing, and poetry.

The Celts celebrated Imbolc in her honor. They would ask Brighid to bring an end to winter and ensure their sheep would have healthy lambs. Since her name means "exalted one," and exalted means someone who is looked up to and held in high regard, she was associated with things that are high up, including flames that rise high into the sky (like bonfires), high mountains, and even high intelligence.

When Christianity overtook the Celtic religion, Brighid was made into a saint whom the Christians called Saint Brigid of Kildare. Saint Brigid is still a patron saint of Ireland, along with Saint Patrick.

Saint Brigid of Kildare

The Morrighan

Celtic meaning: "Great Queen," "Phantom Queen"

Other names: Morrigan, Morrigu, Mor-Rioghain, Badb

The Morrighan was the goddess of war, battles, and fate. She was the one who decided who lived in a battle and who died. She could encourage warriors to fight harder by screaming a battle cry. She is sometimes pictured as a crow, which is why one of her names is Badb (meaning 'crow').

Some records say The Morrighan was Dagda's wife. She was very protective of her territory and would help others defend their land. There are a few sources that say The Morrighan isn't just one goddess but is actually three sisters.

Rhiannon

Celtic meaning: "Great Queen"

Other names: Epona, Macha

Rhiannon is the Welsh name of the Celtic goddess of horses. She appears in a Welsh story called *Mabinogion*. In this story, she marries the Lord of Dyfed, Pwyll, after he chases her for three days on horseback but never manages to catch up with her. Rhiannon was strong, independent, and smart. She represented the strength and grace of horses along with the carefree nature of birds. In *Mabinogion*, Rhiannon has three magic birds who can sing the living to sleep and wake up the dead.

Cailleach

Celtic meaning: "Old woman," 'hag'

Other names: Bheur(ach), Beira

Cailleach was known to the Celts as the Queen of Winter. She was mainly worshipped in Scotland and Ireland. Some stories say she made mountains with a giant hammer to use as stepping stones. She might sound a little scary, but she was the personification of winter. We usually think of winter as dark, cold, and sometimes dangerous, which is exactly how Cailleach was seen.

Some people still tell an interesting legend about Cailleach to tell if there will be a short or long winter. The legend says that on February 1st (Imbolc), if the weather is bright and sunny, it means that winter will last longer, because, on that day, Cailleach is gathering firewood so she can stay warm when she sends in winter again. If February 1st is a cold and stormy day, it's a good sign and means that Cailleach is still asleep and winter will be over soon. This story is the inspiration for Groundhog Day in the U.S.

GROUNDHOG DAY

Groundhog Day. Cute marmot predicts the weather

Chapter 3:
Stories from Celtic Mythology

Most Celtic mythology stories were written down after the Romans took over, so some details were probably changed. The tales in this chapter come from all over Celtic land — Ireland, Scotland, Wales, and France, for the most part.

Celtic mythology stories are divided into four different groups, called cycles. Different groups of Celts, mostly those in Ireland, believed these different cycles. The four cycles are the Mythological Cycle, the Ulster Cycle, the Fenian Cycle, and the Cycle of Kings. In this chapter, we will talk about each cycle and look at a few of the most well-known tales from each cycle.

The first two cycles, the Mythological and Ulster, might be the most famous ones. We'll start with them.

Mythological Cycle

The Mythological Cycle tells the story of the Tuatha Dé Danann, a race of supernatural beings who were basically gods. Tuatha Dé Danann means "folk of the goddess Danu." This story tells us that the Mythological Cycle gods were all children of the mother goddess, Danu (also called Ana or Anu). They were also called Tuath Dé, which means "tribe of the gods." Some of the gods in this cycle are ones we talked about in the last chapter, including Dagda, Aengus (Maponos), the Morrighan, and Brighid.

The Tuatha Dé Danann gods and goddesses are the main characters in the Mythological Cycle. The stories revolve around them and talk about what Ireland was like before Christianity. While there are several stories that make up the Mythological Cycle, we're going to tell you about three of the most well-known tales: *The Book of Invasions*, *The Dream of Aengus*, and *The Wooing of Étaín*.

The Book of Invasions

The Book of Invasions isn't just one story, but a whole book. It's about the mythical history of Ireland and how the Celtic people came to be there. According to the book, six different groups of people settled in Ireland at different times. First there was the Cessair, then the Partholon, the Nemed, Fir Bolg, Tuatha Dé Danann, and lastly the Milesians.

The Book of Invasions might be based on some historical events, but for the most part, it's all fiction. So why is it still important?

For one, it gives us more information about gods and goddesses we might not have known about otherwise. It also shows us just how much Christian influence there was in stories written about the Celts long after the Romans took over the Celts. For example, the *Book of Invasions* says the first group of people to make it to Ireland, the Cessair, were related to Noah (as in Noah and the Ark). Since the original Celts weren't Christians, the story of Noah and the Ark wouldn't have been

33

part of their religion. Once you take out the Bible references, though, *The Book of Invasions* becomes a pretty good record of Celtic beliefs in Ireland.

The Dream of Aengus

If you remember from the last chapter, Aengus was the god of love. *The Dream of Aengus* is how the god of love found his true love.

One night when Aengus was sleeping, a beautiful young woman appeared to him in his dream. When he tried to reach out to her, he woke up. The whole next day, Aengus couldn't stop thinking about her. He couldn't even eat! He hoped that when he went to sleep again he would see her, and he did. This time she had a timpan, which is an Irish musical instrument. She played it very well, and Aengus had the sweetest night's sleep he had ever had.

He couldn't eat again the next day and didn't want to do anything except think about her. This cycle happened for an entire year. When he slept he would see her, and when he was awake he couldn't stop thinking about her. Aengus got sicker and sicker because he couldn't eat. He was in love, but he didn't want to tell anyone because he was embarrassed. The god of love was so lovestruck he was ill!

Many doctors visited Aengus to try to figure out what was wrong, but no one could figure out why he couldn't eat. Finally, a doctor came who took one look at Aengus's face and knew that the god had fallen in love. The doctor sent for Aengus's mother so she could try to take away her son's heartsickness. But the only thing that would cure Aengus would be finding the woman who visited him in his sleep.

Aengus's mother looked everywhere for a whole year, but she never found the woman. She decided it was time to ask Dagda, Aengus's dad, for help. Dagda and Aengus had argued with each other a long time before this and weren't speaking. Dagda didn't want to help, but then he learned his son was sick, so he decided to look for the woman, too.

Dagda was very wise, but he didn't know everything. He knew who to ask, though. He went to King Bodb, who was his son, too. Bodb ruled the Síde of Mumu, which wasn't a place but a group of fairies. Bodb promised to search for the woman for a year. At the end of the year, he found her.

The woman was Caer Ibormeith. She was at the Loch Bel Dracon, which means "Lake of the Dragon's Mouth." Bodb and Aengus went to the lake together to see if Aengus recognized Caer Ibormeith. There were 150 other girls at the lake, but out of all of them, Aengus could see the one he was in love with. He wanted to marry her right away, but he couldn't ask her without talking to her father first, who was the Prince of Sid Uamuin in Connacht, which is a province of Ireland.

Ethal Anbúail, the prince and Caer Ibormeith's father, didn't want Aengus to marry his daughter. Dagda couldn't let his son die of a broken heart, so he threatened Ethal. Then Ethal told Dagda why he couldn't let anyone marry his daughter. Every year on Samhain, Caer changed form. She was a woman for one year and a swan the next. During the years when she was a swan, she couldn't leave the lake.

Swan

Dagda told his son about Caer's transformation, but Aengus still wanted to marry her. Since he had seen her in human form, he knew she would turn into a swan the next Samhain. On that day, he went to the edge of the lake and called to her. She was already in swan form, and she told Aengus that she would only marry him if he promised to let her go back to the water whenever she was a swan. He promised, so she came to him at the edge of the lake. Aengus finally got to hug the beautiful woman he had seen so many years ago. He transformed into a swan so he could be with her on the water. They stayed together for the year she was a swan and every year after that. The god of love had found his true love, and the two of them would be together forever.

The Wooing of Étaín

The main character of this story is Étaín, the most beautiful woman in Ireland. She is the perfect image of Irish beauty, with long red-gold hair, bright blue eyes, and snow-white skin. *The Wooing of Étaín* tells of the two lives of Étaín and the men who fell in love with her.

The story starts with Aengus, the same god of love from the last story. Aengus was raised by his brother, Midir. One day, after Aengus had grown up, Midir went to visit him. When he got to Aengus's home, a boy who was playing nearby accidentally hit Midir in the eye with a sprig of holly. He was cured, but since his injury happened on Aengus's land he asked Aengus for compensation, or payment. What Midir wanted was to marry the most beautiful woman in Ireland, Étaín.

Holly

Aengus agreed, and he set off to see Étaín's father, Ailill. Ailill asked Aengus to do him a few favors before he would let Étaín go to Midir. Aengus had to pay Étaín's weight in silver and gold, change the course of a river, and even clear a large field for planting crops. When he had done everything Ailill asked, Aengus brought Étaín to Midir.

Everything would have been fine if Midir's first wife, Fúamnach, hadn't found out about Étaín. She was very jealous and wanted to get rid of Étaín. She turned Étaín into a puddle of water and thought that would be the end of the other woman. But the puddle of water evaporated, and Étaín turned into a worm, then a purple fly. She wasn't an ugly, tiny fly, though. She was as big as a person's head and beautiful, like a butterfly. Her wings made a pretty buzzing sound, and she could still sing. A drop of water that dripped off her wings could cure any sickness.

Midir saw Étaín the fly and knew it was his wife. She followed him wherever he went, and he happily listened to her and enjoyed her company. In return, she kept him safe and watched over him while he slept to make sure no one tried to hurt him. Fúamnach had thought that if she got rid of Étaín, Midir would come back to her and love her again. When she realized that Étaín was still with Midir and Midir wasn't going to look for another wife, she became so mad that she blew a breath of wind so strong and so powerful that it caught Étaín and swept her far away. For seven whole years, the wind kept blowing and Étaín couldn't find anywhere to land.

Finally, after seven years, she landed on Aengus. Aengus told her that Midir had been looking for her the whole time. She was too weak to go back to Midir, so Aengus took care of her.

Fúamnach found out Aengus was taking care of Étaín and conjured up another great wind to blow her way. For another seven years, the poor Étaín was blown around all over Ireland. When the wind died down, she was exhausted and couldn't land properly. She fell into the cup of a woman named Etar.

Etar didn't notice Étaín, took a drink from the cup, and accidentally swallowed her.

Étaín had changed form before, though, and this time she turned into a baby. After being born the first time 1,012 years earlier, marrying Midir, turning into a fly, and being swept away for a total of 14 years, she was reborn as Etar's daughter. Her first life had come to an end, but her second life was just beginning.

After Étaín had grown up again, she received another offer of marriage from a king who wanted to marry the most beautiful woman in Ireland. The king's name was Eochu Airem. He needed a wife because no one would respect a king without a queen. The moment he saw Étaín, he fell in love with her and married her right away. The problem was, Eochu's brother, Ailill, also fell in love with her. Just like Aengus had in the previous story, when Eochu's brother fell in love he became very sick. Eochu left on a trip, and Étaín stayed behind to take care of Ailill. Every day she stayed with him and tried to nurse him back to health, and since he was in love with her, it worked.

When he started to get better, Étaín asked him what had been the problem in the first place. Ailill finally admitted he was in love with her. He was getting better, but he wouldn't be completely healed unless she would agree to run away with him. She didn't want him to die, so she agreed. They decided to meet on a hill behind the king's house that night.

When Étaín arrived on the hill, she saw a man who looked like Ailill. He said he was too tired to run away, so Étaín went back to the house. She saw the real Ailill inside and realized the person she had met on the hill had been a stranger. The next three nights, she went to the hill intending to meet the real Ailill, and each night someone who looked like Ailill but wasn't, was there.

On the last night, Étaín finally asked who the person was and why he was in disguise. The man finally revealed his true face, and it was Midir! He had found her after all that time. Étaín asked why she had been sent away from him, and he told her about everything his first wife had done. Fúamnach was now dead, so it was safe for Midir to bring Étaín back home.

Étaín had been born a new person, so she didn't remember Midir. Midir said he would do anything he could to get Étaín back. He even cured Ailill of his lovesickness so Étaín wouldn't feel like she had to take care of him anymore. Étaín told Midir if he could convince her new husband, Eochu, to let her go, then she would leave with Midir. She thought if Midir could convince Eochu, then she would know for sure that she was the same Étaín who had been married to Midir in another life.

Midir could perform magic, but he had to win back Étaín fair and square. One day, he showed up at the king's house and challenged Eochu to an old Irish board game called Fidchell. Their first wager was fifty horses. If Eochu won, Midir would give him fifty of his best horses, and if Midir won Eochu would have to give up fifty of his horses. Midir was good at Fidchell, but Eochu still won. Midir kept his promise and brought fifty horses to Eochu. He then challenged Eochu to another game

41

of Fidchell, this time with a different wager. Over and over again they played the game, and every time Midir lost and had to pay up.

One of the last bets they made was if Midir lost, he would have to build a road over an impassable bog. A bog is a place where the ground is muddy and wet. The ground is soft and can't hold up anything. Midir lost the game and had to build the road. It was very well made, and Eochu was happy. Finally, Midir knew it was time to make the bet that he had been waiting to make since the first game.

Bog with trail and lake in Clifden

For their last wager, Midir asked for a kiss from Étaín if he won. Eochu agreed, since he had won every game before then. This time, though, Midir won. Eochu told Midir to come back in one month, and he could have his kiss from Étaín.

Eochu never intended to let Midir have a kiss, though. A month later, he locked up his house and had it guarded by his best warriors. Midir was able to get into the house anyway. He accused Eochu of going back on his word, and since there were others around who might think Eochu was a bad king for lying, he agreed to let Midir have one kiss from Étaín.

When Étaín appeared, Midir grabbed her around the waist, turned them both into swans, and they flew off together.

Ulster Cycle

Also known as the Red Branch Cycle, the Ulster Cycle is all about fighting for honor and glory. The main and most important story, *Táin Bó Cúailnge*, is also called the *Cattle Raid of Cooley*. The Irish hero known as Cú Chulainn is a brave warrior and protector of his people in this story, and he just might be the best-known hero in Celtic legend. Have you ever heard of Hercules, the Greek hero? Well, Cú Chulainn, is the Irish version of Hercules. Let's take a closer look at the story of his life and learn why he means so much to the Irish even to this day.

Táin Bó Cúailnge

The story *Cattle Raid of Cooley* starts with Queen Maeve and her husband King Ailill. They were talking about things kings and queens like, which is mostly money and riches. Maeve and Ailill were comparing what they had brought into the marriage, such as clothes, gold, animals, and so on. They were adding up how much everything they owned was worth, and so far, they were 100% equal. That is until Ailill mentioned his prized possession, a strong white bull.

Maeve wasn't the kind of woman who could let her husband one-up her. She decided that, in order to remain equal with her husband, she needed to own a bull worth just as much (or more) than her husband's. There just so happened to be one bull that fit that description.

The Brown Bull of Cooley was far superior to Ailill's bull. When Maeve found out about it, she was determined to have it. She sent one of her messengers to the Daire of Cooley who owned the bull. She offered to give a large piece of land and fifty cows if she could borrow the bull for just one year. Surprisingly, the Daire accepted. He even threw a party for Maeve's messenger and the other men she had sent. That's where everything went wrong.

Brown bull

One of Maeve's men told one of the Daire's servants that it was a good thing the Daire gave in. Otherwise, Maeve would have taken the bull by force. The Daire overheard this conversation and immediately kicked everyone out. He sent a messenger back to Maeve with a new message. Instead of accepting her deal, if she wanted the bull she was going to have to take it from him. Talk about an overreaction.

Maeve was never one to back down from a challenge. She gathered together her strongest fighters and set off for Cooley. This is where the hero, Cú Chulainn, comes in.

Cú Chulainn was a warrior fighting for the Daire of Cooley. He was part of the Red Branch Knights of Ulster. As the knights were preparing to meet Maeve's army, they were all struck down by a magic spell. Every single knight became deathly ill. Everyone, that is, except Cú Chulainn.

All by himself, Cú Chulainn faced Maeve's army. He single-handedly faced her toughest warriors and defeated them, one by one. He had killed one hundred of her best men when her last warrior stepped forward. Ferdia, the last man standing, was Cú Chulainn's best friend. They weren't going to fight, but Maeve told Ferdia that Cú Chulainn accused him of being a coward. Ferdia couldn't let his honor be attacked, so he fought his friend.

Ferdia and Cú Chulainn were evenly matched, so their fight went on for three days. Crowds started to gather around them, cheering. Cú Chulainn was distracted for one second, and Ferdia saw his chance. He quickly stabbed Cú Chulainn with his sword. Cú Chulainn's chariot driver threw a spear to Cú Chulainn, and he stabbed Ferdia with it. Cú Chulainn didn't die, but Ferdia did. After Maeve pitted the two friends against each other, she took advantage of the distraction of their fight and stole the Brown Bull of Cooley.

When Maeve returned home with her prize, she put the brown bull in the same pen as her husband's white bull. The white bull didn't know who this newcomer was, so he challenged the other bull to a duel. The two fought long into the night, until finally the brown bull defeated the white bull. After he won, the brown bull ran home to Cooley. He wasn't used to so much fighting, though, so the moment he got home he fell over and died.

After a long battle, a cattle raid, and a bull fight, Maeve and Ailill were both just as rich as the other was.

The story doesn't end there, though. Cú Chulainn was still alive, and Maeve blamed him for everything that had gone wrong with her plan. She wanted revenge, so she had three magic spears made which she gave to Cú Chulainn's enemy, Lugaid. Then she had a goblin place a magic spell on Cú Chulainn that would make him hear war sounds in his head. Cú Chulainn thought his home was being attacked, so he grabbed his chariot along with his chariot driver, a sword, and his horse.

When Cú Chulainn reached Lugaid, Lugaid picked up the first spear and threw it. The spear missed Cú Chulainn and hit his chariot driver instead. The next spear also missed but hit Cú Chulainn's horse. Finally, the last magic spear found its mark. It hit Cú Chulainn in the side, and he knew it was fatal. He tied himself to a pillar, faced down his enemies, and stayed like that for three whole days. His enemies were too afraid to go near him because he didn't seem to be scared, even though he was going to die. After three days, a raven landed on Cú Chulainn's shoulder. Ravens are birds of death, so everyone knew that Cú Chulainn had died.

Tragedy of Deirdre

Deirdre is sometimes called "Deirdre of the Sorrows." Not a very happy name, is it? Deirdre's story is a sad one. She is referred to as a tragic heroine, which means the things that happened to her prove she's brave, but she doesn't get a happy ending.

The story starts with a king, Conchobar Mac Nessa, and his harpist, Felimid. Felimid's wife was pregnant with their first child. The king had a druid working for him who agreed to tell Felimid a prophecy about the baby. After placing his hands on Felimid's wife's belly, he foretold the baby was a girl who would grow up to be the most beautiful woman in the world. Felimid thought this was a good thing, but the druid warned him that too much of anything is a bad thing. Too much beauty could lead to danger for the child. Then the druid told the king the baby would split the Red Branch. The Red Branch in this story is the same as the group of knights in the last story. The king's men panicked and said the king should order the baby be killed.

Conchobar was a kind king, and instead of killing an innocent baby he told Felimid he would raise the child in his home, keep her safe from everyone else, and if she was as beautiful as the prophecy said she would be, he would marry her. If the king married her, no other man would have the guts to look at her.

When the baby was born, she was named Deirdre and sent to live with a nurse named Leabharcham, who was very protective of Deirdre and cared for her like she was her own daughter. No one else except the king and an old man who brought food for Deirdre and Leabharcham had ever seen the girl. No one knew about her beauty, which is exactly how everyone wanted it to stay.

One day, though, the old man brought meat for Deirdre and her nurse. He dropped it in the snow, and a raven swooped down to get it. Deirdre fainted, and everyone thought it was because she saw blood on the meat. Deirdre wasn't that weak, though. She told Leabharcham when she saw the color of the blood, snow, and raven all together, she fell in love. She decided that the man she would marry had to have raven black hair, pale snow-white skin, and rosy red cheeks. She didn't know if there was a man who fit that description, but Leabharcham did.

One of the king's warriors, Naoise, had hair, skin, and cheeks exactly as Deirdre described. Leabharcham couldn't lie to Deirdre, so she told her about Naoise. Deirdre was desperate to meet him, but Leabharcham knew how dangerous it would be. She also knew Deirdre was supposed to marry the king.

Deirdre wouldn't listen, though. She begged and begged to be allowed to see Naoise. Leabharcham couldn't take Deirdre to him, but she could bring the warrior to the two of them. She invited Naoise and his brothers, Ainnle and Ardan, to hunt near where she and Deirdre lived. When they arrived, Deirdre peeked out of the house to see if she could spot Naoise. When she saw him, she knew he was the one she had to marry.

Leabharcham begged her not to leave the house, but she couldn't stop the determined girl. Deirdre ran out to greet Naoise, and he fell in love with her the moment he saw her. He knew who she was and that he couldn't marry her since she was supposed to marry his king. When she learned he wouldn't run away with her, Deirdre placed a magic spell on him that forced him to agree. They couldn't stay in the kingdom, so Deirdre, Naoise, and Naoise's brothers set off for Scotland.

The four of them lived in Scotland for a long time. They stayed in the woods so no one would see Deirdre. The brothers hunted for food, and Deirdre made a nice home for them all. For a while, they were happy. But the brothers missed Ireland because it was the only home they had ever known. Deirdre was happy in Scotland because she knew she was safe there.

Meanwhile, the king was furious that one of his own warriors had taken off with his bride-to-be. The king's foster father, Fergus, kept trying to calm him down and get him to forgive the brothers so they could come home. The king wouldn't agree for a long time, then finally he realized he looked silly holding a grudge for so long. He told Fergus he could go to Scotland and bring the brothers home, if he promised to keep them under his protection. Fergus agreed and set off for Scotland.

While Fergus was on his way, Deirdre had a dream. In the dream, a raven flew over from Scotland to Ireland. The raven had three droplets of honey in its beak that turned into blood when the raven landed in Ireland. She knew this dream was a warning not to go back to Ireland.

Rraven

The next day, Fergus arrived in Scotland. He called out from the beach three times. The brothers all heard him. With the first shout, they knew it was an Irishman. After the second shout, they could tell it was someone from their home of Ulster. The third shout told them for sure that it was Fergus. Deirdre tried to convince them all not to go, but since Naoise was leaving, she had to go, too. When they got back to Ireland, though, they realized the king hadn't really forgiven them.

The king first wanted to know if Deirdre was still as beautiful as she had been before running away. When he found out she was, he became jealous and ordered his Red Branch knights to kill Naoise and his brothers. Half of the warriors refused, and half followed the orders of their king. Just like the prophecy foretold, the Red Branch was split in two.

Naoise and his brothers were all strong fighters, so none of the king's men were able to defeat them. The king realized his plan wasn't working, so he asked his druid for help. The druid didn't want anyone to die, so he made the king promise not to kill the brothers. If the king accepted an apology from Naoise instead, the druid would help. The king promised. The druid cast a spell that made water rise up around the brothers. They had to tread water to keep from drowning, which tired them out. When they dropped their weapons, the druid dropped the spell.

Now that they were weaponless, the king's men grabbed them. The king said he had promised he wouldn't kill them, but meant someone else could. He promised a reward to whoever killed the brothers, but no one wanted to do it. Finally, one person agreed to do it. He was the King of Norway's son, and Naoise had killed his brothers and father in a battle a long, long time ago.

Naoise and his brothers were inseparable. They all begged to die at the same time so none would have to live without the other. Naoise had a sword that could cut through anything, which he gave to the King of Norway's son. With the sword, the man killed all of them at once.

Deirdre had seen everything, and she promised to hate the king forever. The king tried everything to win her back. He gave her a beautiful home, sang to her, and sent her presents. She closed the window when he sang, sent back all the gifts, and ignored him whenever he was around. The king finally got tired of her rejecting him. He knew the only person she hated more than him was the person who had killed her true love. He told her if she wouldn't agree to marry him, he would send her to the King of Norway's son to live with him for a year.

Deirdre knew the king was trying to bully her into giving in, and she was not the type of person to give in to bullies. She refused, so he put her in a carriage and sent her off to the only other man she hated. On the way, the carriage passed sharp and dangerous cliffs. Before anyone could stop her, Deirdre jumped out of the carriage, hit the sharp rocks, and died.

She was buried next to Naoise, but the king didn't want them to be together even after they had both died. He had stakes of wood buried between the graves to separate them.

The stakes of wood grew roots, though, and those roots grew into two beautiful trees. The two trees twined together over the graves and became a symbol of never-ending love.

Twisted heart tree

Fenian Cycle

The Fenian Cycle is all about the Fianna, a nomadic tribe of outlaws. The cycle's hero is Fionn mac Cumhaill. Most of the stories in the Fenian Cycle involve hunting and adventures. The first story you'll learn from this cycle is how the hero, Fionn mac Cumhaill, became the leader of the Fianna.

Fionn and the Fianna

A bard named Finnegas trained Fionn in the art of singing and poetry. One day he caught the salmon of knowledge, which is a salmon that has eaten a hazelnut (the nut of knowledge). While he was cooking the salmon, he burnt his finger. By putting the burnt finger in his mouth, he gained all the supernatural knowledge the salmon had.

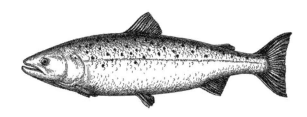

Salmon

Later, Fionn learned about hunting and other skills of a warrior from Aengus, the god of love. After he had been trained by a god and a bard, he decided it was time to find his family. He set off for the land where his uncle lived. He was able to find it by chewing on his thumb, which still held the knowledge from the salmon. His uncle wasn't part of the Fianna anymore, but he told Fionn he should try to become one of them or even the leader. With this advice, Fionn set off for the High King, Goll Mac Morna.

Fionn arrived at Tara, the High King's home, on the night of Samhain. What he didn't know was that for the past few years, the king and his men would have a big feast, fall asleep at the tables, then wake up to find Tara on fire every Samhain.

When Fionn learned about this event, he decided to figure out what was going on. In order to stay awake, he did something very clever (but dangerous). He rested his head against the point of his spear, and whenever he would start to fall asleep, his head would press harder on the point and the sharp pain would wake him up. His method was very effective, and he was able to stay awake all night.

Eventually, he heard a weird noise. It was like singing, and it was the noise that had put all the men except Fionn to sleep. Fionn followed the noise and saw the hill next to Tara opening up. A creature that breathed fire came out of the mountain, still singing its song. Fionn used his cloak to put out the creature's fire breath, then chopped off its head.

When the creature was dead, the king and his men woke up, figured out what Fionn had done, and came out to congratulate him. Goll Mac Morna realized Fionn was strong, brave, and fit to be a leader. He gave over leadership of the Fianna to Fionn.

Fionn was a good leader who made one big change when he took control of the group. Every man who wanted to be part of the Fianna had to pass a test. Fionn made it even harder, but he went through the test himself just to prove it wasn't impossible.

The first test involved making a man jump over a branch higher than his head and run under a branch lower than his knees. Then the Fianna would tie the man's hair into braids and chase him through the forest. While running, the man couldn't snap a twig, scare a bird, let his hair come out of the braids, or let any member of the Fianna catch him.

The next test involved digging a hole as deep as the man's waist, putting the man in it, and making him fend off the rest of the Fianna with nothing but a stick. Everyone else had their swords, and if his hair came out of the braids or he were cut, he would fail.

If a man could pass these tests, next he would learn 12 books of poetry and recite them all from memory. The last steps were to give up ties to any and all family members, promise to never seek revenge if someone killed them, and marry a woman for love, not for her money.

Cycle of Kings

The last Celtic mythology cycle is the Cycle of Kings, or the Kings' Cycle. You've probably guessed by now that this cycle focuses on kings and their lives. It talks about what kings are supposed to do and how to be a good king. Some of the kings in the Cycle of Kings stories really existed, but not every tale about their lives is true. We're going to tell you about Cormac Mac Art, who was considered the greatest out of every king Ireland had ever seen.

Cormac Mac Art

The story starts with Cormac's father, Art, and another man named Lugaid Mac Conn. Art and Lugaid both wanted to be king, and both had a right to be. They decided to figure out who should be king by fighting. On the way to the fight, Art talked to a wise man who told him he needed to have an heir before he died. Art didn't have a wife or any children, so the wise man let Art marry his daughter. Art went off to battle and died, but Achtan, the daughter of the wise man, was pregnant with a son.

Achtan knew Lugaid would try to kill her son if he found out she was pregnant, so she went off in secret and was going to let a friend of Art's raise the baby. On the way, she went into labor and had to have the baby in the forest. She was so tired after having the baby that she fell asleep, and so did the nurse who was with her. While they were sleeping, a mother wolf came along and took the baby. Everyone thought the baby had been killed.

Wolf

Many years later, a hunter found the mother wolf and followed her back to her den, where he found the human baby who was now a toddler. He knew right away the child was the lost baby, so he brought him to Lugna, Art's friend who was going to raise him when he was a baby.

Lugna named the baby Cormac and raised him as his own son. But one day Cormac learned Lugna wasn't his father and asked about his parents. Lugna told him he was the son of a High King and he could claim the throne if he wanted to. Cormac decided to try, so they went off to Tara, the home of the High King.

One of the duties of the king was to settle legal arguments and decide on punishments. When Lugna and Cormac got to Tara, they saw the king was deciding what to do about an old woman whose sheep had eaten the queen's plants. The queen wanted to take all the sheep, but the old woman had nothing else.

Grandmother feed the sheeps. Snowy winter day.

Lugaid Mac Conn, the king, agreed and was about to make the poor woman hand over the only things she owned. Cormac saw what was happening and suggested that instead, since the plants would grow back, the old woman should give the wool from the sheep to the queen, not all the sheep themselves. Everyone who heard Cormac speak realized he was the son of a king and was wiser than Lugaid.

The people of Tara wanted Cormac to be their king instead of Lugaid. Lugaid saw he was beaten and gave up without a fight. Cormac became the king, and he was the kindest, wisest, and best king that Ireland had ever known.

The Melusina Story

The last story you'll learn doesn't fit into any of the cycles. It probably comes from the French Celts.

In the story, Melusina's mother was a beautiful fairy who lived in the forest. The King of Albany saw her while he was hunting and asked her to marry him. She agreed, but on one condition. The king wasn't allowed to come into her room when she was giving birth to any children they would have, and he couldn't come in when she was giving the kids a bath. He promised not to do either, and they were married.

Melusina's mother gave birth to triplets, all girls. The king had forgotten about his promise and came into her room, so she left with her daughters. They went to Avalon, which is a mythical island.

When the girls grew up, Melusina asked her mother why they lived on Avalon. Her mother told her what had happened, and Melusina decided to punish her father for breaking his promise. She and her sisters put their father in a mountain along with everything he owned. When their mother found out, she was angry. She made the girls let their dad go, then she punished each one.

Melusina's punishment was the worst since it was her idea and she was the oldest. Every Saturday, Melusina would turn into a serpent from the waist down. The punishment wasn't too harsh, but it was very inconvenient.

Echidna

Conclusion

The Celts may be gone, but their descendants are still around, and they still tell the stories of Cormac Mac Art, Fionn, Cú Chulainn, and the Tuatha Dé Danann. In Ireland especially, the land and culture are alive with stories from the past. If you ever get a chance to visit Ireland, take a minute to appreciate that long, long ago there were people living there who believed in strong, powerful gods, fairy folk who were sometimes up to no good, and all sorts of supernatural beings who lived alongside humans.

There's still more to learn about Celtic culture than what we covered in this book. Look up pictures of the amazing shields they created, find out about symbols like the Celtic Cross, and learn about the tribal gods and goddesses we couldn't get to.

Ornate Celtic cross (Knotted cross variation n° 3)

Even though the surviving Celts eventually converted to Christianity, their culture lives on. When you look at a swan, think of the god of love and how much he went through to find his own true love. When you see a fly, think of Étaín and everything she suffered, only to be reunited with her love in the end. These don't have to be just stories. They can inspire you to be as brave as Cú Chulainn, as good a leader as Cormac Mac Art, and as resilient as Étaín.

More from us

Visit our book store at: www.dinobibi.com

History series

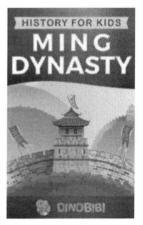

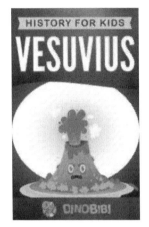

Travel series

Made in the USA
Las Vegas, NV
17 December 2020

13725737R00042